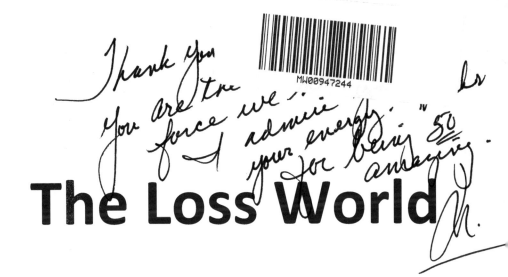

The Loss World

A culmination of thoughts and musings edited from the journals of Mary London Szpara September 6, 2004 through September 6, 2012.

A journey of survival through hope.

Mary London Szpara

Dedication

When confronted with extreme situations, compartmentalize.
It helps isolate the whole into small parts.
Grasp the little pieces instead of trying to take hold of the complete
picture.
It's a survival mechanism.

No matter how sick Michael was,
or how bleak the outlook,
I never really had anything except hope.

I guess that is just how I am wired.
Look at what is immediately in front of me,
and work with it.

That is where these words came from: survival.
I needed the outlet to get through the process of grief without being
swallowed up by it.

This is dedicated to my beloved husband
Michael Wayne Szpara

We had one rollercoaster of a ride baby.
In hindsight-
I'd still do it all over again with you.

CONTENTS

ACKNOWLEDGMENTS

Thank You

First and foremost, I thank God, the Creator, for His overwhelming love for me. I thank Him for leading me to a place in life those many years ago where I met Michael and learned what the gift of love between soul mates could be. I thank Him for the lessons I had to learn, despite the fact that they were difficult, because they made me stronger.

I thank Mary, the Mother of God who shows me every day what the true strength of being a woman is. It is not in being strident, it is in learning the lessons, not blaming God, and moving toward the ultimate reward.

To Bet & Walt "Mom & Dad S": You raised an amazing son who honored you and became a beacon of light to so many who were afraid. His love of people and God was something taught at home. I know you saw his strength through the final years, and guided him from above and were well pleased.

To my Parents: Dad, I think you are appreciating Michael like never before now that you have more one-on-one time with him. Mom, I think my strength comes from Grandma through you. It's a blessing and I am grateful.

I thank our family by blood: Siblings, In-laws, cousins, Aunts & Uncles, nieces, nephews: Each of you : special.

I thank my dear Carolina Family, especially all my "Sistas". Too many to mention. You know who you are. I love you dearly. You may see your names within the pages...I didn't ask permission, but I know I did not need to. Without you here: life would have been darn near impossible. You helped me to laugh when I never thought I would smile again. And you made me find my humor in the most unusual situations.

To all of Michael's friends, Marc, George, James, Ed & especially Cousin Jim: you knew just how special he was...and that he made a difference in each of our lives. Thank you for keeping me in yours.

To my special "big sister" and her husband: Gladie & Chuck Schommer: You embraced me throughout my life, and when I met Michael, you welcomed him in just because I loved him. That was enough for you. You made every effort to connect with him, and in the end, the bonds that were made will always be remembered. Thank you for being there through the years. You are cherished. No one else could appreciate Tin Can Mary & Michael on the Mantle as fully.

The Loss World

Mary London Szpara

PRELUDE

I cuddled with him for the last time on a Monday

It was Labor Day...we had the whole day to spend together.
It started out so well.

I woke up with the sun working its way through the clouds. Its occasional appearance caused raindrops on the window to glisten in the dawn light. It rained pretty heavily overnight, but the sky had cleared and it looked like it was going to be a nice day after all.

I turned over and reached out to touch him...he had been having trouble sleeping during the night. I woke him several times, as he sounded so congested throughout.

He was sleeping soundly and curled as usual on his left side.

I moved my hand up to touch his head. I loved his hair. Although he was 58, it was beautiful....the kind most women, including myself, envy.

Soft and light brown with a touch of silver and wonderful gentle curls. I loved those curls. I let one twist its way around my finger for a moment before it glided gently off.

I smiled, knowing how much he hated the curls and the silver. He had just enough vanity to have gone to the hairdresser a few weeks earlier to have her add some highlights. The color made the silver a bit more blonde. He wore it fairly long. I thought with or without the silver, he was still the most handsome man in the world. After all, he was my Michael.

My Beloved Michael.

I fell back to sleep in our "spoon" position, as I so often had in the past. I slept an additional two hours and when I awoke he was no longer in bed. I rolled over and called my friend and neighbor Debbie to confirm our appointment to take a walk that morning.

"it is a bit misty out there" she said when I asked if she wanted to get started.

"We won't melt" I replied. It was about 9:45 am, and she said she'd be up in a bit. That meant I had about 10-15 minutes to get ready.

I let the dogs out for their morning constitutional in the enclosed side yard, then headed toward the bathroom to brush my teeth, where I found Michael standing in front of the commode.

"I'm nauseous", he told me.

"Do you want me to get you something darlin'?"

"I think it must be something I ate...maybe those shrimp yesterday: all those onions. I just feel sick"

I noticed he was a bit unsteady. "why not sit down for a minute, you look a little rocky."

He sat on the commode and looked at me with his incredible puppy eyes. "I just feel sick"

I felt the panic rise: "is it your liver?"

"No, it's not that. Sal is ok."

"Do you want me to stay here, should I call the doctor?"

He smiled weakly and comforted me with "No, it's ok, I'll be fine once I throw up. I need to throw up. Just promise you'll cuddle when you come back in"

"OK"

"Promise?"

"I promise"

I kissed his forehead and headed out, as the dogs (which we referred to as our 'dog-bells') made enough noise outside to herald Debbie's arrival.

"I'll be back in an hour LB" I called

"Remember you promised to cuddle when you get back"

"I look forward to it."

"Have a good walk with Debbie, I love you"

"I love you too"

4

I grabbed my shoes, headed out the front door, where I sat on the rocking chair on the front porch to put them on.

"Good morning Mary" Debbie sang out as she climbed the front steps. "I brought an umbrella just in case."

"Doesn't look like we'll need it"

"So, how are you this morning?"

"Good. But Michael isn't feeling too well. He said he's nauseous. He thinks it's something he ate yesterday."

"is he ok?"

"I don't think its anything to be concerned about. He didn't seem very upset. He just made me promise we'd cuddle when I got back."I laughed, shaking my head. "Not like he has to twist my arm."

Debbie smiled.

We went for our walk.

It took us about an hour, a normal walk for us. When I returned, I glanced into the bedroom and he looked as though he had fallen back to sleep. I smiled to myself as I noticed he had returned to his usual position on his left. Not wanting to wake him, I decided to get the side yard trimmed before I headed back to bed. I was sweating from the exercise and thought I might as well continue sweating and finished the small bit of mowing I had abandoned the night before. It would only take a few minutes and then I could take a bath and rejoin Michael in bed as promised.

He and I had been busy doing lawn work the day before - a Sunday afternoon. He was on the riding lawn mower, and I used the push mower to trim a bit closer to some of the plantings. He was done before me and went into the house. It wasn't long before he came outside with a twinkle in his eye to talk me into quitting before work was totally completed, insisting I stop exactly where I was, to put the mower under the trees in front.

He was in his totally charming mode, which I could never resist. It was part man, part child and completely engaging. "Bargain Hunt is on, I made us a picnic, the bed is waiting".

Picnic in bed. One of our favorite events.

Something we started early on in our relationship after weather interrupted a planned outdoor escape to Charlottesville. When we later moved to Montana, it became a weekly event every Sunday. Broasted chicken and picnic in bed.

The practice continued in New Orleans and again when we moved to the Carolinas...until he became ill, and he had just recently begun to find that part of himself again. The playful, sweet and funny man that I had lost for several years due to liver disease and the meds that followed had returned.

How could I resist him?
I thought how wonderful it was to have him back: how blessed I was to love someone so much and know I was cherished in return. I agreed, willingly, the child in me rejoicing.

We picnicked, then began watching the internet as the hurricanes began to get more active.

He had become my personal meteorologist over the years. Fascinated with weather patterns, the internet was his virtual playground into forecasting. Our good friend Ed often called just to get an update on what to expect before he went out to play golf. He often joked Michael could tell him the exact time to expect the storms to arrive.

That evening, and into the early hours of Monday morning, Michael was busy tracking the hurricane heading toward our friends near Daytona Florida. It had been an active hurricane season, and he was worried about whether they would be hit. I was working on an art project nearby and we bantered back and forth until we were tired as we concentrated on each of our projects.

We went to bed knowing our world was safe and quiet for a while. The storm would be heading our way later in the week we were sure. I had no idea a whole new type of storm was about to blow through my life.

That Monday morning, there was little work left to do and I started the mower up quickly to zip the remaining patch. As I finished, the dogs started to bark. The biggest culprit was Rex, our male Australian Sheppard. Rex, also known as Bubba, was deaf, and sensitive to everything around him. I looked at him in the dog run, and he was staring up at the house, barking frantically non-stop.

"Knock it off Bubba" I called to him. Smart move. As though he could hear me. His sister Mikki started up with her high-pitched yelp and our

German Sheppard/hound mix Maxx joined in for a full-on dog cacophony.

"Enough guys, you'll wake your daddy!" I told them   They kept barking, which was really unusual as they never made a big fuss when they could see me and I was near. I looked into their area to see if another animal had gotten in to cause so much stress.

As I did, Rex charged the gate. I had not secured it properly when I had been in there earlier and he popped the latch up. It opened, in a flash the dogs were on the loose. Mikki and Maxx quickly rushed out, ran up to me barking, then whirled around and headed toward the woods. They were gone.

Rex took a fast lap around me, around the front yard, then headed up the front steps and jumped on the front door.

"OK Bubba, good boy! You didn't leave the yard, let's go in."

I opened the door, and he headed back to the bedroom. It was totally out of character for him. Being a creature of extreme habit, he normally would head straight for the big leather chair in the living room.

This time, he went directly toward Michael's side of the bed. He took up his position right next to him, sitting on his haunches.

"He wants you to get up and pet him. Tell him what a good boy he is for not leaving the yard LB" I said as I walked down the hall.

I continued talking as I made a quick left into the bathroom to turn on the faucet in the tub.

"Hey sweetie, I stink. I am hitting the tub before I climb back into bed OK?"

I walked into the bedroom to make sure he had heard me.

"I promised I'd be back to cuddle, just give me a few minutes to clean up LB. Hey, LB, wake up"

I reach out to touch his toes, grabbed his foot with my right hand and shook it.

"Hey LB, Bubba is right next to you, and wants some attention."

He must have been playing possum...no reaction.

"Hey, LB, wake up"

I shook his foot again and something odd registered in the back of my mind. I looked at him more closely.

My heart skipped a beat.

He look so sweet and serene lying on his left side with his hands under his cheek: but something wasn't right. I could feel it, and a cold terror started to move up my torso.

"Oh Mikey. Please wake up."

No response as I shook him harder.
I reached up and shook his shoulder. His head, which was cradled on his hands lolled to the side.
"oh no Mikey. No, no ,no no no Mikey."

Somehow I knew he was gone.

I reach for the phone, dialed 911, then Debbie.

'Debbie, its Michael...please come"

I don't remember exactly what she said, but she said she would be there right away.

I turned him on his back and check his pupils. Fixed. I opened his mouth to see if he had had a seizure and bit his tongue, while at the same time I was searching for a pulse. No swollen tongue, no bite marks, nothing except his gums had no color and were slightly blue.

NO no no no no no no no no no no no Mikey. Nonononononononono

Oh God, Please. Not Yet. Not now.

His lips were turning pale. That much registered. The cold feeling continued to move through me and settled in my chest. I wanted to be sick, I couldn't.

I started CPR. I wasn't sure if there was a pulse or not, as mine was racing. I knew I would be able to at least breathe some air into his lungs to prevent brain damage if he wasn't breathing.

Debbie arrived in mere moments and she said "I'll do the compressions". She took those over as I continued to try to breathe for him.

The sound of an ambulance came down the road.

"Rex must be put outside on the porch, I don't want him to get upset and bite anyone" I told Debbie.

Rex had moved from his position directly next to Michael toward the foot of the bed. He was on "guard duty"

"Come on Rex", she said, "let's go outside."

He refused to budge. He had decided his job was to sit there and protect Michael. Debbie had no choice but to pick him up physically and set him on the back porch. Or was it me? I don't remember that detail well enough.

The first responders had arrived.
They came in, asking questions I don't even recall. The only thing that made an impression was when I asked if he was gone.

"yes"

"How long"

"It's been a while"

"How long"

"I don't know"

At that moment, two other people arrived, this time with machines.
They put the contacts on his chest to run a tape, looking for a heartbeat.

"Anything" I asked.

"No, Ma'am. Do you want us to resuscitate?"

"Is he gone?"

"Yes Ma'am he is"

"How long has it been"

"Its been a while. Do you want us to resuscitate?"

9

"I have health power of attorney. We have DNR requests. Can you tell me you can get him back without having any brain damage?"

"No Ma'am, we really can't"

"No. No. IF he can't be fully Michael- you can't...we promised each other......"

Somewhere inside my head a whirring sound began. I sat beside Michael, then lay down next to him, cradling him in my arms.

"Shhhhh...I'm here....I promised we'd cuddle....I'm here....I promised."

I cradled him as I dialled the phone.

"St. James"

I called our church. Father Ed answered.

"Father Ed, Its Mary Szpara"

"Hello Mary, how are you?"

"Not good Father, its Michael."
"What's wrong with Michael?"

"He died Father. Please come. He needs the blessings."

"What happened. Where are you?"

"He was sick earlier. He went back to bed. He didn't wake up. I'm at home."

"where do you live?"

"Brother Darryl knows the way."

"He's not here right now."

My mind, on autopilot, gave him directions.

I held Michael as I picked up the phone to call our dear friends Ed and Carolyn.

"Ed its Mary."

"Hi, watcha doin"

"Ed, its Michael"

"What's wrong!" I heard the panic in his voice. "is he ok?"

"No, he's gone."

The pause was heart stopping.

"What!" Disbelief in his voice.

"Ed, Michael died. Can you please come over."

Carolyn could be heard in the background, "What's wrong?" "Michael's dead".

"WHAT!"

The rest of the conversation escaped me, I just knew I heard them saying they would come. I hung up the phone.

The EMS men were standing quietly by.

'we need you to leave the room for a while. We have to examine him."

I extricated myself from around him. "Don't hurt him. I'll be right here. I'm coming back in when you're done. You cannot leave him alone." I locked eyes with one of the men there "I don't want him alone" "He won't be alone. We'll get you when we're done"

I walked down the hall past the bathroom where the water was still running in the tub. It was up to the rim of the claw foot tub. I reach over, turned off the faucet, then plunged my arm into the tub to pull the plug. The water was cool to the touch. I stood up and wiped my arm off with a towel, then headed back down the hall toward the front of the house in a daze.

People were coming in the door. It was Ed and Carolyn. The look of shock was written on both of their faces.

"what happened!" Ed had lost all color in his face. Carolyn and he both reached for me at the same time.

"Oh God! He's gone!" I said as I was enveloped in their embrace. I was numb. My mind stopped registering much of anything.

I noticed Carey, a neighbor in the room. Her eyes were filled with tears. "Oh Carey, We couldn't save him this time."

She put her arms around me and we clung to each other. Nearly 8 years earlier, Carey had responded to a call for help. Michael was ill, waiting for a liver transplant, and was at home alone. I could not reach him from work, he did not answer the phone.

I called another neighbor who had keys to the house. Their 15 year old daughter Errin answered. I asked her to go across the road, get Carey, and let her in the house to check on Michael. I did not want Errin to walk into a situation that might find her face to face with death.

Carey had called me from the house. Michael was in a coma on the floor and she had called 911. I talked to the EMT's, found out which hospital they were going to, and hung up the phone. Carey was instrumental in saving Michael that day. Now nearly 8 years had passed, Michael had seen supposedly insurmountable challenges and met them head on. Today, there was no way to save him. The odds had won.

"I came over as soon as I saw the ambulance", she said. "I'm so sorry."

A flurry of activity began in the house. Friends and neighbors began to wash the dishes in the sink, sweep the kitchen floor.

Carolyn asked me whom I needed to call. I picked up the cell phone and started going through the phone book, reading off names and numbers. The movements were automatic. I could feel a flush move through my whole body, and I kept gasping for air. I couldn't breathe...there was not enough air in the room. This was all just a bad dream, and if I just do all these things, make all the right decisions, and do everything I needed to do, the dream would be over, I would wake up and everything would be ok. It had to be ok. It had to be a dream.

It wasn't a dream.

This was Reality 101, and I was about to have a crash course in the education of a lifetime. Life was the instructor. There were no text books or study tools. I was strictly "winging it". Gulping for air, my mind reached for the basic information I needed to sort out my thoughts.

The EMT's informed me they were finished, and I could go back into the bedroom.

I climbed into the bed and held Michael close. I just wanted to hold him as long as I could. I had to hold him. I needed to hold him. Everything else around me faded into the distance. The people coming in and going out. The voices in the other room.

Only one thing was important right now. Michael & I . It was always just the two of us.

We were team Szpara. We relied totally on one another, and were not just husband and wife, we were best friends and soul mates. There was no "me" and "you" there was "us". That was the way it had been for over 25 years. We were almost inseparable after the day we met nearly 26 years earlier. Our 25th wedding anniversary was just a few weeks away, although we had been celebrating the event all year long. It was a huge mile mark, not just because of his health, but because in this day and age, we were not the norm but the exception.

There were times when we were apart over the years. When Michael was working out of town, or had gone to see his dear Aunt Helen. But we spoke to each other at least once a day. A night never went by that we did not tell each other we loved one another. And now I could only hold him, rock him, and tell him I loved him as I waited for Father Ed to arrive.

I called our close friends Glenda and Walter. Walter was also a liver transplant, and he had been fighting cancer the past few years. His cancer was winning. We had recently learned that hospice was at their home.

Michael had taken that news badly. He loved Walter dearly, and just 3 days before we had gone to First Friday mass because it was so important to him to receive the blessing of the sick and pray for Walter. We were expecting a call from Glenda any day: she was not expecting a call from me.

When Glenda answered the phone, I registered her expression of disbelief. I remember her asking me where I was. I told her "in bed, holding Michael". Her response was so reassuring. "Good, that's important" she said more, but I don't recall words, just the feeling that she approved, and knew that I was doing the right thing for us. Her shock was evident and I know her next big task would be to tell Walter. But my task at hand was simple, just to hold my love in my arms until they had to take him away.

We had set up our funeral wishes 2 years earlier after Michael's father died. We decided to get the basics out of the way. It would be done. Nothing to occupy precious real estate in our brains.

The sheriff's department had arrived, and one of them called the funeral home. They asked if I wanted an autopsy. I said "no, no more cutting. No more surgery. No." Not unless they had any questions about why he died.

Nothing looked out of place. No trauma. No questions raised. We did not have a doctor there to pronounce. They did call one of his doctors (he had so many) and they were satisfied with what he had to say.

All these things to do that make our leaving this earth nice and tidy for the legal eagles.

All I wanted to do was tell them to get out of the bedroom and leave us alone. Those moments I would be able to continue to hold him were ticking down, and I wanted more time...just a little more time...just a few more moments...

I stroked his hair, smelled it, inhaled his smell. He always smelled so good. Even after working out. He was fastidious about his personal hygiene, and his skin had this wonderful comforting smell. I inhaled deeply and closed my eyes...rocking back and forth...holding onto him for dear life.

Father Ed arrived and came straight back in to the bedroom. His kind eyes were filled with sadness and questions. "What happened?"

I had been thinking about that as I sat and lay next to Michael, and I knew in my heart that the answer was so clearly displayed earlier.

"His heart Father." His heart.

All the drugs had taken their toll. All the signs that it was his heart were there, but he had just been to the VA the week before and nothing was said about his heart. He didn't ask. He had x-rays taken of his back. He was having back pain, and was afraid he had cancer in his spine. He did not tell me of his fear until the results of course. No Cancer. I remember how happy he was to declare that. The pain in the back was something else entirely, it was quiet and deadly , and we never saw it coming.

One of the meds Michael had been taking was constantly spiking his potassium levels. The lab was always upset, worried that his heart would stop. It was something to be concerned about, but something he

14

always told me not to worry about. I was always worrying about him, and the potassium was just another thing to make me nutty.

The interesting thing is, the past few months I had begun to let most of my fears go...and the last few days were perfection. God was definitely watching out for us. He let us have the most perfect last few weeks. They were indeed more wonderful than I could imagine. The worry was there, but not in the forefront...it was more subdued, as though we had a handle on things and everything would be all right.

Not quite. Nothing would ever be right again. Life had changed forever, and although I knew it would happen someday I still thought we had beat the worst of it...that we still had more time.

No time left.

The clock was ticking. Father Ed blessed Michael. I told him about the dogs and our deaf dog. Father said they saw the angels and Our Lady come to take Michael home.

I believe that. Michael was so devoted to Mary, the Mother of God. He and I always went to Perpetual Help devotions on Monday night. It was only right that this Monday, Mary would come to bring him home and repay him for his love toward her Son.

That comforted me, but most of all, I knew it was the truth. Michael had a love for Jesus that was so complete and so pure it epitomized the innocent belief of a child. I know that is what drew many in the parish toward him. They sensed that childlike faith. It was remarkable. His faith made me see my own in a whole new light.

There was something so beautiful about it, even now, I can close my eyes and see that glow he had about him when he talked about God. He always said God had more for him to do 7 ½ years earlier. That is why He let Michael live.

Michael never took that gift of life for granted although he carried with him so much guilt for being a survivor.

He received 3 organs, outlived his mother, then his sister and finally his father.

He was the last of his immediate family and that was difficult for him to fathom. He loved them whole heartedly and the tragic loss of his sister was especially painful. As every brother and sister they had times when they disagreed. But as brother and sister the bond was unshakable.

Blood is thicker. The last words they spoke were "I Love you". Her death rocked his world in so many ways. He fought so hard to live and her loss was so incomprehensible.

He was left to carry on the family responsibilities. His father had Alzheimer disease. The person that was his Dad was gone, even though he looked the same. The shared memories were erased and someone else, from another time, had taken residence in his father's mind. Some of the things he said and did were really quite funny and Michael was able to see the boy his father once was. He eventually found joy even in that sadness. It happened after he talked to one of his dad's nurses after a long visit. Michael told her he was upset because his dad did not remember him. She told him "he did not forget you Michael. For him, he is a boy, and you were not born yet." That statement gave him the ability to see God's hand in a whole new light. Michael's faith pulled him through his personal losses, but his guilt as a transplant recipient was difficult. He lived because others had died and donated their organs for transplant.

Surviving those who gave him new organs and the loss of his family was a burden he carried with him. He didn't dwell on it, but it was something we both had to work through.

He was a survivor. He loved me and he lived and survived longer than the odds would have given him. I know it was his love for me that kept him going as long as he did. He loved me with his emotional heart, loved God with his spiritual heart, but his physical one, was just too beat up.

The barrage of drugs he needed to survive also hastened his death.

I sat in the bed, holding him, rocking him, until the funeral director came into the room and said, "we can take him now".

"No" my brain and heart cried. "No, he needs to stay here with me" But my head kicked in long enough for me to realize that they needed to take his body away. They took my friends aside, told them to take me outside while they prepared Michael for travel.

I knew what they were doing, trying to distract me. I thought at the time how kind they all were being to me, but we were all just operating on shock. I think sometimes that I was the strongest one there that day.

Until Paula arrived

My friend Paula was, and is, a rock.

She spent more time with Michael and I over the years than most. She knew him better than any one of our friends in North Carolina, and she loved him like a sister. His feelings toward her were mutual. Paula was family in every way to both of us. When she needed advice about life, or work, or anything in particular, it would certainly not be unusual for her to talk to Michael. She respected his opinions and the way he would cut through the crap. And there was so much crap to cut through sometimes. But Paula would be the first to tell you he would look at her, cock an eyebrow, pull her over to the side and say "what were you thinking!" She loved him for that, and like me, he just loved her-for her. She had a heart of gold and I cherish her every day.

Paula's girls, Jessie and Jackie are twins. They drew pictures for Michael when he was in the hospital and Paula brought them to him 8 years earlier. Michael always told her he would focus on their artwork to keep his sanity when he felt his mind leaving him due to another bout of encephalopathy.

Paula, a wonderful God fearing West Virginia girl, had all the vim and vinegar that was required to survive life. She was brutally honest and the most loyal friend any person could ask for. She was, and remains, a blessing to me in so many ways. Her sense of humor gave me relief when I needed a smile. We shared so many experiences as we both worked in radio early on. Paula was much more the wild child than I, and we both survived some pretty intense party days. Her personal early struggles were part of what made her so strong.

She was at the hospital every chance she could get when Michael was in residence there. When he came home, she brought him "critters" to put outside in the yard.

She brought her huge personality into the house that Monday morning and took charge. "oh honey" she said to me. I let go...and my mind began its quiet shutdown.

Paula and Debbie had gotten together at one point to decide they would take turns staying with me. They didn't want me to be alone, at least not immediately.

I guess everyone was afraid of what I would do. The stress load had been tremendous for over 8 years. How much could someone take?

But I knew God would take me in His time, not mine. Although, anytime He wants me I am ok with that. I have had an amazing life. Suicide was not my problem, but breakdown was always a possibility...or perhaps just shutdown.

I don't remember the remainder of the day. I know I spoke with my mother. She lives in Wisconsin.. Mothers and daughters always have their own way of dealing with each other and we had ours. I told her about Michael, she said she would inform the family. Having lost my father just a few years earlier, I could feel her empathy and I knew I could depend on her to take care of the chore of notifying immediate family.

The remainder of that Monday was gone in a blur. I recall little of it as shock set in. But I had no time to dwell on what had occurred, I had much to do at home. I compartmentalized and began to write an obituary. I wanted it to honor Michael, and his service would be 11 days after his death. I needed time to prepare, to put together my thoughts and my efforts to make his funeral an event that would truly celebrate his life and his eternal life.

We talked often about what we wanted when we died.

Michael said "no tears and negative thoughts. I want this to be a party. When I die I will be ok. God gave me so much and I know what to look forward to. I'm not afraid to die and I want everyone to be happy for me, to celebrate."

So a celebration it would be.

The church was filled with caring people. Six of my seven brothers were there. My sister and her husband had driven my mother down earlier in the week, and left days before the service.

When I arrived at church Michael's sweet cousin Jim was there waiting for me. He was my direct connection to my husband and I clung to him. I needed him there more than I can ever explain. The pain in his eyes almost matched my own. Our loss was shared and I felt his silent strength beside me as I carried the urn containing Michael's ashes down the aisle.

Our amazing and talented friends Robin & Tony Rogers sang Michael home, and as I heard Robin's voice singing "It's a blessing", "Unconditional Love" and the other songs, I heard Michael clapping, and then saying in my mind "well where is the 'Hip Shakin' Mama!: this is a party people!"

His presence was felt as the service started. The flowers by the altar turned over twice, until I said out loud "Michael, behave yourself". He listened, and the flowers became still. A little comic relief was just his style.

The tropical storm from the hurricane had arrived outside the church and I could see the trees whipping around outside through the windows.

After the service, we went into the church basement where friends from hundreds of miles away came to share their grief. His doctors and nurses came up to me with tears in their eyes as their own shock had not registered this as real.

The sky cleared and the storms quieted long enough for a trip to the cemetery where taps were heard along with the sound of gunfire as Michael received his military honors. When the last gunshot echo faded, the last prayer at the gravesite was said, the skies opened and the tears came down from the heavens in sheets.

Cousin Jim headed back to Atlanta, and I headed home with my brother Andy driving. Michael's urn with his ashes clasped tightly in my lap. I was taking him home to be with me. The urn was large enough for us both, and it would sit on the speaker in the living room (where else?) until my ashes would be combined with his. My thoughts were on that moment though-our final ride home together. His celebration at home would begin soon.

Earlier in the week I had traveled to South Carolina for a full trunk load of fireworks.

I wasn't sure if the weather would cooperate, but our Creator was aware of the importance of the day and by nightfall the storms had left the area, and the skies were already clearing to show a few stars.

My brothers welcomed the chance to make some noise and they took control of the fireworks display, set to a music song track my friend Jack kindly assembled for me. The music was part of Michael's life story. Our story together. Nothing like rock and roll and pyro.

I knew he was getting a kick out of it.

As the final notes from Judy Collins "Amazing Grace" hung in the night air with the last of the fireworks floating through the sky, a tear escaped and Sarah, Jessie and Jackie hugged me and watched as a warm wind brushed my face. Michael was with us, with me, drying my tears.

When the music was over, my brothers, mom, aunts, niece. nephew and friends departed. I was left with the cats and the dogs to find a way back to normal…

The Loss World is a culmination of thoughts from the journaling I began after Michael's death.

It is my hope that those who have suffered great loss will be able to connect. To know that someone else has lived through grief, moved through the pain and grown stronger.

It is my wish that if it makes you sad, if it makes you cry, it may also make you smile and believe that there is grace and beauty and love that never leaves us when someone we love dies.

The words from St. Paul to the Corinthians , Chapter 13, 1-13 are often heard at weddings, but these words should also be stressed at times of great loss to bring hope and light into the darkness. I read this passage at his funeral:

"If I speak in human and angelic tongues, but do not have love, I am a resounding gong or a clashing cymbal.

And if I have the gift of prophecy and comprehend all mysteries and all knowledge; if I have all faith so as to move mountains but do not have love, I am nothing.

If I give away everything I own, and if I hand my body over so that I may boast but do not have love, I gain nothing.

Love is patient, love is kind.

It is not jealous, is not pompous, it is not inflated, it is not rude, it does not seek its own interests, it is not quick-tempered, it does not brood over injury, it does not rejoice over wrongdoing but rejoices with the truth.

It bears all things, believes all things, hopes all things, endures all things.

Love never fails.

If there are prophecies, they will be brought to nothing; if tongues, they will cease; if knowledge, it will be brought to nothing.

For we know partially and we prophesy partially, but when the perfect comes, the partial will pass away.

When I was a child, I used to talk as a child, think as a child, reason as a child; when I became a man, I put aside childish things.

At present we see indistinctly, as in a mirror, but then face to face. At present I know partially; then I shall know fully, as I am fully known.

So, faith, hope, love remain, these three; but the greatest of these is love"

The Loss World.

The place where deep sadness,
intense grief,
and overwhelming emptiness dwell.

A numb mind amidst the chaos of emotional turmoil,
where it hurts to move your hand across the bed
because you know there is no human to encounter…

where that empty space is a void so large you are engulfed
by it.

The loss world has become my home.

The Cocoon.

When I was young, I remember being told that God never
gives you more than you can handle.

Intense events and situations can cripple.

But God insulates us.

Surrounds us in a huge cocoon.

It's rather strange to be there…
but it is also comforting.

No matter how overwhelming things are,
I absorb, and observe only little bits and pieces of it at a
time…
never the complete picture.

A little window opens up for just a brief moment in that shell.

A rush of intense emotions are allowed to pass through and
inside.

The window closes,
and I am isolated again.

It is as much as I can handle,
and I don't handle much too well at all these days.

The Sigh.

Sadness has reached a new level.
It is so overwhelming, even tears cannot do it justice.

Instead: I sigh.

It is deep, lonely and total.

A manifestation of grief that it is beyond crying.
Breath knocked out of you in a continuous cycle.

You find yourself in a vacuum.

Then you notice the uncontrollable shaking of the fingertips.
Nerve ends so affected that the trembling takes on its' own
life.

The sigh is loud.   Unstoppable.

It occurs when the emotion becomes so overwhelming that
you don't think you can move.

It is the only time when you can truly feel:
but the feeling is so total,
that you can do nothing more than just be.

A contradiction, certainly.

An intense experience that lasts only a breath,
but one that takes your breath away each time.

We've all heard it
-or seen it without recognizing it-
until it lands at our doorstep.
Then it becomes familiar.

Incomprehensible reality made simple.

The Hole.

Who chiseled this hole in my chest?

Who opened up my soul and scorched it with a flame so hot
that I have become numb?

Who made it so difficult to breathe that each breath is a sob?

Who put that ringing sound in my head…
that buzzing noise in my ear?

How can I possibly feel so much more hollow than empty?

I can't bear it. It's too empty without you.

And my love,
if you can't come home,
please come to me in my dreams.

I want to feel.

The View.

I look at life through a hazy glass and from a distance.

Emotional nerve endings are felt singly as they fray.

But that feeling too,
is from a distance.

A direct hit will shatter my fragile fortress.

A poem,   a song,   a movie,
a phrase,   words,
even a look.

If the outlines of the message become distinct,
a crack starts to form.

The fissure is deep.

The temptation is to fall.

The need to close my eyes and have you magically reappear
is staggering.

The Silence.

All the sound in the house is deafening.

No TV.   No radio. No music.

No snoring.

No laughing in your sleep.
No gasp from pain.
No moan from passion.

No sound escapes your lips
because you are not here.

I listen for your voice.

I hear it, far away in my head
"LB to LB krrrrrrrrkkk, come in LB."

"I love you."

"When you get back,
you have to promise we'll snuggle."

"You promise?"

"I promise"

"I love you"

LB to LB, krrrrrrrkkk, come in LB.

The Pictures.

I surround myself with them.
Looking for the perfect expression that says
"Michael."
Your love as seen through the camera, into my soul.

Making composites of the two of us together,
because we were,
but one of us was holding the camera,
therefore only single shots now exist.

Must remedy that.

We were never single: always a unit.
So many pictures, but never enough.
I could wallpaper a room with your face.
Your sweet smile. Your dancing eyes. The look of love.

Perhaps a life-size standup would be better.

Or perhaps worse.

It could not hold me in its arms.
The hand could not reach out to touch my cheek.
It could not cuddle with me in the middle of the morning,
or the end of the day.

It would not be warm.

It would not be real.

It would be you, but not You.

It would never be enough.

The Crack.

I talked to someone on the phone today.
They were only concerned with their agenda.
I could not stop myself from wanting to scream.

I wanted to start to yell at them: tell them they were ignorant.
The world had stopped for me, I was crumbling into small
little pieces.

But they weren't aware of the complete and utter despair that
engulfed me.

In my eyes they were not only guilty of unawareness, but of
not caring.

I had labeled them void of humanity, and after hanging up
the phone, I sank into total meltdown.

My legs could not support my body,
my sobs could not drown out the screaming in my head
"no, no no no no no no no....."

The crack widened, as I sank to my knees,
biting on my hand to stop myself from losing all sense of
reality.

It feels like an eternity since I started crying,
but eternity was too short a time frame.

I heard the sound of my voice change as the sobs
deepened.

It sounded, and felt, raw...

inhuman.

Zippers and Buttons.

I put on a dress today that made me cry.
Not because it reminded me of a special occasion.
Because it showed me how easily I took all the little things
for granted.

I put on the dress, and began to zip it up my back.

I stopped at the point I could no longer reach then I said
"honey....." and stopped.

I pulled the dress off, sank down into the bed and the tears
began to flow.

It was just a zipper...but you would always pull it up the rest
of the way. It was a part of our routine.

Even if I could do it myself, it was just something we DID.

Something you did for me.

You would zip my dress the rest of the way up.
Then place your hand in the small of my back.
It was a loving, gentle touch.

"OK, all done."

I miss your hand on my back.

Zippers or buttons in the back.

The reminders of the simple things that made US special.

Little things,

that are huge.

Beauty.

I can hear your voice. We were getting ready to leave for a wedding. You looked at me, told me how wonderful I looked. How beautiful I was. How much you liked what I was wearing…how much you admired my legs.

The dress had a slit up the sides. I picked it because I knew you would appreciate it. You loved my legs.

You noticed my shoes.

"You look like Cinderella in her silver slippers".

Oh my Prince Charming. How handsome you were that day. Your suit was a perfect fit. The lavender dress shirt gave your eyes a deep glow. Your hair was soft, touchable, with a gentle unruly curl in the back.

You were my handsome Prince, and I always felt beautiful in your eyes.

Even on my worst day you made my life beautiful.

Now when I dress, I imagine you looking at me.

I check the view in the mirror,
as though it was through your eyes.

I dress for you my handsome Prince.   I dress for you.

Oh, and by the way,

I just bought another pair of killer heels you would love.

Things.

I find myself wanting to buy things.

I have this uncontrollable urge to spend, spend spend...

Who cares?

You can't take it with you.

But it is just stuff.

Stuff I don't need, but it fills the space around me.
It temporarily fills that hole inside.
Like a finger in a dam.

Damn.

The hole is getting bigger…

enveloping me…

Pulling me in,
then pushing me down.

The 'things' are meant to prop me up.

It doesn't work.

I know why I do what I do.

I am so empty without you to fill that void.

The Closet.

I just can't help myself.

I have to go into your closet.

I gather your shirts in my hand
Bring it to my face,

and breathe deeply.

I just can't get enough of your smell.

The last shirt you wore is bundled in the drawer near the
bed.

You cling to this life in the fibers.

Each deep breath brings you nearer…

I close my eyes when I breathe.

I fool myself into believing that you are within reach.

I feel the cloth,

not your skin.

But the smell comforts me more than anyone else can.

The Top Shelf.

I bought a step stool today.

There were some things I kept just out of reach.

Not because of children,
because we had none.

Not because the things were dangerous, or toxic,
or because I wanted to hide them.

They were just items I did not use often…

Molasses, corn syrup,
the good dishes…

The things I had on the very top shelf in the cabinets are
now strangely out of reach.

Actually, they always were,
It is just that you used to be the one to reach up to get them.

OK, you were not taller than everyone, just taller than I

You would always say
"don't climb on the counters…you'll fall"

Now I move a stool over to the cabinets and must use it to
reach,   or I do what you told me not to…

I climb

and I fall…

there is no one to catch me now,

I am always bruised,
not just from the falls.

"honey, I can't reach it" echoes in my mind throughout the
room.

You liked that…

Just like "Honey, could you please open this jar for me?"

I struggled with it first, and then you popped it open right
away…

you always said "well, you loosened it for me."

Sweet, our simple way of courting one another after all these
years.

Were we each capable of doing it ourselves?

Sure,

But it was so much better when we shared the little things.

Somehow, a stepping stool just is not the same.

One more minute.

Just one more minute…
one single 60 second span of time…
one revolution of a second hand around the dial…

One more minute.

To dance, to kiss, to pray.

To Be: Together.

Just one.

Only one minute: 60 seconds-
a simple request.

An impossible request, but a request never the less.

Just one more minute to gaze into eyes that expressed a
soul.

A minute to last the rest of my life…

the test of my life.

Just 1, or 2 or 3…
I'll take 10 seconds…less.

But, oh what I could do with one more minute.

Echoes.

There are echoes around me…

Echoes of your voice

Echoes of our life

Echoes of our laughter

Echoes of our love

There are moments when I feel as though I could reach out and physically touch those echoes, and they would materialize…

that you would appear and my world would suddenly right itself again.

But then I pull my hand back, because if you do not appear, the disappointment would be too intense for me to handle today.

Perhaps tomorrow…
Or next week, maybe next year…

Well…maybe in two years….four….twenty….

For now, it is too early to test the waters.

I don't want you gone, and if I listen to the echoes, you are within reach…

My hands remain in my lap,

but I touch you with my heart and my mind.

Job.

Job was tried by God and not found wanting.

God gave him so much: for which he was thankful.

When Job lost everything, he was thankful for God's love.

God was so good to us my love.
He gave us each other.

For that I am so grateful.

God left me with memories…
I think the memories are here to remind us of God's strong
love.

I am thankful for His love. I am eternally grateful.

I look forward to eternity with you…with God.

Wait for me,
I may be a while.

And please ask God not to test me too much…

I really suck at dealing with things right now.

Recordings.

It was a bad day.

I was going through my dresser to sort through the bits and pieces I threw into a side drawer. As I looked at each item that was dated when you were with me, the tears became sobs that racked my body and I called out to you.

"I need you. I Love you. I miss you so"

And you heard me. There is was:
a tape with your voice on it.

You were singing "you are my Sunshine",

Only you had changed the lyrics.

It was our little theme song and we sang it to each other often. It was silly, and sweet.

When you were sick, you stopped singing. Could not even remember the lyrics, or recognize the melody.
But then one day when you were in the hospital,
I came home to find your voice on the answering machine.

Once again you sang to me. I heard the lilt in your voice.
The smile in your eyes was magically transmitted through the phone.

It made me warm. It gave me hope.
I recorded the message because I feared not hearing you sing it again. It was labeled and put into a drawer.

I needed you today…I called out for you.
You answered with our song.

You made me happy, when skies were grey.

In Case of Emergency.

I bought a new wallet today. Inside was the ID card.

"In Case of Emergency Please call…"

Who?

Who gets the call now? A friend? A family member?

Who?

How many names must I write down there…
Should I put 1, or more…

Should I list at least 3, since they all live separate lives from
me and may not be easily available…

Do I just list my brothers, or my sister, all whom are far
away, or do I just leave it blank?

Not because no one cares, because so many do
But they all have their own lives

And some just would not be able to handle the stress of an
emergency.

In the event of an Emergency…

For now:

Just call God,

let Him sort it out.

With this Ring.

I still wear your ring.

Not just the wedding band you placed on my hand the day
we were married,

But your wedding band too.

It is on the middle finger right next to my wedding band.

Side by side
Just as we walked through life.

I can clink them together when I move my fingers

They communicate with each other
With us.

With these rings

We are still wed.

58 forever.

It was my birthday today
I'm another year older

You'll always be 58.

Although you were 10 years older than I
Someday I will càtch up with you

I feel the panic rise in my chest

In nine 9 years we'll be the same age

I cannot conceive that

Somehow I have managed to get through each day

Those steps are minimal

But to live beyond you

It's too impossible to imagine today

Celebration Blues.

Our 25th Anniversary
I woke up this morning with that thought ringing in my head.

"Happy Anniversary my Love" I spoke to the empty room.
It was a milestone for us.

Partly because no one in my family thought we would make
it past 5 years much less 25. I joked with Dad one day,
asked him if they placed bets on how long we would last...
he giggled.

Yup, the only ones that knew we were perfect for each other
were us.

Even after heath issues arrived - every extra day was a
bonus. Nearly 8 years of bonus time after your transplant.

But today was the big one.

25 years as Husband and Wife

We got so close to getting here together.

Just weeks away.

Nearly 11 months ago you proclaimed this to be

"Our 25th Anniversary Celebration Year"

It was as though you knew more than you were telling

Or perhaps we both did.

We counted the time but pretended we didn't

Train songs.

I needed to work off some of this sadness:

Habitat had another house to roof.

Good plan.

I climbed the roof and looked into the clear blue skies of
Heaven.

"Hi Darlin' : I promise to be careful"
I said to you and myself.

Then a train passed by
The whistle sounded

Then another

And another.

You loved the trains

It was a whisper of love, not just a whistle

Train songs bringing your kisses through the air.

Not once

Not twice

But 3 times

Good things come in threes

US.

There was You   There was Me

Then there was US

We still remained You & Me
But the US was the rock I always knew I could depend on.

It was bigger It was better It was whole.

I miss US
I miss WE
I miss OUR

Everything I have and do and feel
will always have US in it.

You are a part of me, Therefore
WE Will do things together

There is no ME without You attached.

All that I will ever have is Ours.

Colors.

The sky was blue and so am I

The sky was red, so are my eyes

The sunset is the color of the way I seem to feel,

And I feel lucky I can feel at all.

My heart is bleeding tears for you
The rain starts to fall

The day is gone, so are the arms that held me close.
The night is black, as the shroud that covers me
I find that hope, has lost its way
I find that I, am losing mine.

Your love was like a warm summer day
Inviting, and wonderful, I sought your sun

Your love is still in my heart,

but I'm lost and I'm needing you home.

She loves me yeah yeah yeah.

Today I received a message from you.

OK, it was from a friend, But it was straight from you.

Jimmy & Eva came by today.
It was the first time I'd seen them since you died.

Jimmy told me he would tease you about why I put up with you and you'd say, "Because she loves me Jimmy!"

He said it with such joy.

The nuances were perfect: I could hear your voice.
I saw a twinkle in his eyes, the same one I saw so many times in yours. The playfulness. The sweetness.

The joy that was you.

When they left his final words to me were

"she loves me Jimmy"

He just wanted to tell me that.

He thought I needed to know

Thanks for the message
I do love you

Yeah...Yeah...Yeah

Better some than none.

It is getting close to Christmas and somehow I am finding the
Joy you have given me throughout the years, fill me with
Hope for a future that will bring peace

I can talk about you -
without bursting into unbelievable bouts of tears.

But I still have an empty hole that only you can fill.

I find myself ok with being alone
Because I can talk to you at any time
And still feel the love you gave me.

I would much rather have that love for the time we had
together

Than never have it at all.

No Anger.

I want you to know I'm not mad that you left

I am only grateful you are not in pain.

I told you a long time ago that when your time came:

You had to promise to haunt me.

Well, I feel you here-

But I need you to become a bit more active

Work on that would you?

Bear in a Bag.

He was hanging on the back of the backroom doorknob.

We kept him there for a reason.
He was a little bear In a little paper bag

The words "I'm Sorry" were written on the bag.

He was our little peacemaker

When we argued, (many times we had no idea where or how
it started, much less what it was about)

It may well have been me or you to start the fuss - it didn't
matter- and the Bear did not judge.

He just waited patiently for one of us to pick him up, walk
contritely up to the other and present him

It always did the trick, for we knew that it must be done with
a whole heart

Contrite and loving.

I picked him up and dusted him off.

He's not seen any use for a long time.

I placed him out of reach, but within sight.

A reminder of compromise - A promise of forgiveness

Hmmm, the world could use a Bear in a Bag.

Wow! What a way to achieve world peace.

Questions.

I have so much to talk to you about and so many questions to ask.

I still start a sentence thinking you are in the next room. But you're not.

I miss our daily talks

In the morning, your silliness

Your unbelievable "sales pitch" to get me to do what you want.

(I have to admit, your negotiating tactics really were amazing)

Your touch

Your intelligence

You

I even miss our arguments:

Because making up was always the best part

And I realize it was ok to argue-

We learned to listen.

No one ever listened to me like you.

I'm still talking…thanks for listening.

Christmas Eve.

Extreme highs

Extreme lows

Can you say depressed?

I recognize the signs.

Today it hurts more
It is harder to accept than most days.

I look at our tree and I am aching to hear your voice as you
admire and comment on the decorations made over the
years.

I so desperately want to hear you say "I love You" and tell
you the same in return.

My best gift would be a wonderful dream tonight

I would like that more than any gift that money could buy.

It will be my prayer at church

For Joy

For Peace

And

A Dream of You.

Christmas Day.

The birth of the Christ Child
A beautiful event

I went to midnight mass, just as we had last year

The choir was awful… it was so bad I started to laugh
silently, my head down (most appropriate)

Everyone thought I was crying because you weren't there.

Someone even patted my shoulder.

That made me laugh harder…
(the need to snort was unbearable: but I managed to refrain)

I heard you laugh with me...
in me

My mind flashed with a distinct picture of that glitter of
"trouble" in your eyes.

I heard your voice saying

"Oh God, make them stop!"

I prayed for Joy

God gave me laughter.

Thanks God

I needed that.

The Waning hours.

The last moments of our last year together are slipping away. I opened a bottle of champagne we were to drink together some day.

Now is the day, it's the last day of our last year
The final minutes and seconds are counting down.

I am more than just tipsy, it's all I can do to remain focused on the clock as it ticks. I want to stare it down, to will it to stop, to make the hand move backwards.

It defies me, and mocks my desires.

I have no wish to be near people to celebrate anything. I just want to sit here and reflect…Regret

Reflect on the kisses we shared. Regret that I did not kiss you more. Reflect…Regret

Reflect on the laughter and joy.
Regret that I did not record your voice and laughter to play back in the quiet dark night. Reflect…Regret

Reflect on the final weekend we shared. Regret that it could not have stretched on forever. Reflect…Regret

The clock strikes 12

I'm lost in the melancholy sound of the striking chime.
My heartbeat feels the rhythm and pleads it to stop

The hand moves to 12:01.

Why am I still here?

Moving Forward.

Someone said I must "Move On"

Oh please.

SHUT UP

Moving on is a negative.
It is something you do when you divorce,
when you lose a job, when you quit

It is not what you do when you lose your love
Your Soul Mate - Your partner

You just try to move FORWARD.

Today, I am just standing still - Not moving at all.

It hurts to move. I think I may break if I take a step, but I'll try

Maybe a tiny one…a little itty bitty one

Whew!

Now just breathe

Stop telling me to move on. Other people can move on.

Or better yet: Move away from me.

Me: I'll just try to move forward: Forward is positive
It means I take you with me. It means I won't abandon life or
love or you

Forward is a possibility…tomorrow.

Much more will be asked.

I was in church this past week. Father Ed's sermon included
the following: "those whom have been given much: much
more will be asked of them"

My heart broke in two and the tears flowed.
I felt as though he were speaking of you and me.
We were given so much: An incredible love for one another.
A love of life, The ability to touch others

The Gift of life

The gift of more time together when we thought it was lost.

Much was asked

You were given a huge challenge, you stepped up to the
plate and knocked it out of the park.

You took the cards you were dealt, played the hand through-

Helped those along the way

You survived with dignity and grace

Much was asked

The task was now mine to take up the challenge step up to
the plate - knock it out of the park

I need to play the hand I'm dealt
And learn to survive with dignity and grace

Much is asked

Dumb and Dumber .

I needed to probate your will. The thought was daunting to
say the least. But Sweet Carolyn said "I'll go with you".

We took the trip to the courthouse, walked into the clerks'
office, stated why we were there.

I felt the earthquake inside. How do I possibly hold it
together? After all, this act would make your death real.

Carolyn understood and became an emotional shoulder to
lean on should I crumble and fall.
But it seems God was in a very playful mood that day.

The women working in the office were, well to be kind: a few
bricks short of a full load.

They proceeded to search for the proper forms, explaining
the person that normally did it was away. Their bright smiles
wilted as they discovered what would usually take a few
minutes became a hysterical study of ineptitude.

Carolyn, the quintessential lady, was quite proper in
appearance, but she wasn't fooling me. I could see her
grinning out of the corner of my eye, and more than once I
found myself clearing my throat and biting my lips, as the
laughter bubbled beneath the surface.

Apparently a typewriter was not something either of the two
ladies were familiar with.

Whiteout became their best friend.

When asked "aren't initials required where you make
changes? " I asked innocently. The response was of

puzzlement. (Perhaps the vapors from the extensive use of the corrective fluid affected their grasp of legal matters)

We left quickly as the barely contained laughter burst through our lungs and escaped in the crisp fall air when the courthouse doors closed behind us.

Carolyn's eyes met mine and the tears glittered as we grinned in delight at the sheer silliness of it all.

It was the worst of times, but became a "best of" day.

The blessing of smiles among the tears, shared with a friend.

Humor found in the most inappropriate places.

1 year gone.

Annette knew I needed a distraction today and she provided it with a trip to a flea market for the day.

Creating a new memory to help heal the old. She knew I needed to find a way through.

It was a day of smiles and laughter, but at the end it was still a night of reminders, of disbelief.

You can't be gone.
You won't be gone
You'll never be gone

The simple fact remains:

You will always be here

As long as I breathe-Your breath shall be my breath

My heartbeat - Shall be your pulse

I look for your smiling eyes in the quiet of dusk and I find it in the gold and green and brown hazel sky tones

I hear your voice calling me - whispering through the pines…Then its' gone.

Each day I survive without you
Is one day closer to seeing you again.

Fireworks and Forever.

It's the anniversary of your death.

I bought fireworks earlier in the week - just as I had when you died.

As the sky darkened I walked out to the side yard to light them

Through the open windows I heard the strains of "Wish You Were Here"

How appropriate.

The fireworks soared into the skies as the tears streamed down my face.

"I love you and miss you and need you so much"

I think I said the words aloud. If not, they were loud in my mind.

The last of the sparkles glittered into the heavens with my message and then disappeared.
The sound of the phone ringing at the end of the sky show propelled me back inside

It was one of our neighbors.
You never got to meet them, but they have become dear to me.

Their oldest son William wanted to call me after the fireworks.

"it was beautiful-I loved it!" he said.

A tear joined those already in place on my cheeks.

His mother picked up the phone and I heard a tender note in her voice. There was something Gloria needed to tell me.

She said William asked her;
"Momma, why is Mary shooting fireworks?"

She told him;
"Mary is doing that to let Michael know she loves him"

She said he was quiet for a moment. William was a thoughtful and sensitive young child…then he responded:

"He will love it. It is so beautiful he will want to come home and stay forever"

Out of the mouths of babes.

You always ended your notes to me with "forever plus one day"

How appropriate that William used that word.

William's words brought you home to stay with me today…

And forever…

…..Plus one day.

Roses & Chocolates.

Today, it was all I could do to rise from the bed to get dressed.

Another anniversary without you.

I had a Mass said for us this morning. I thought about every moment of that past day as I drove to the church.

I found peace there in our pew. It was easy to imagine you here with me, because I knew you were.

I saw the sad smiles from our friends at Mass. Their tears matched mine, but none of us spoke.
Words were unnecessary
I could read their eyes, and they mine.
When I arrived home, I realized just how much you wanted to celebrate the day with me.

As I walked in the door I smelled Roses and the Chocolates.

It startled me at first.

The smells enveloped me when I opened the door.
Not a flower or morsel of chocolate was anywhere to be seen

I walked outside to see if it was a mind playing tricks, but when I came back into the house the scents were stronger than ever.

I knew you would not forget this day.

Thank you for the roses and chocolates my love

They were wonderful!

People Think.

People Think I should be angry with God
Because He took you away from me.

It is not anger that I feel What I feel is so alone…

so alone

I hear your voice within the darkest of nights
I see your face, I feel your touch in my dreams.

I think that you are just a heartbeat away-

Won't you Stay…
won't you stay when my eyes are open.

And when the sun does decide to rise

I feel its warmth- just like the love from your eyes

I know you'd be home if you could

I don't blame my dear Lord
Because He only wants the good ones,
and you were the best I could find.

So forgive my tears Lord,

But it is what I have to do.
My heart is still breaking, Its shattered and blue

And if You want me now, I would gladly say yes

Because Home is where You are

And my Darling now rests.

Home School.

Leaving home is hard, but staying there without you with me:

Is heartache

But its comfort too - Because it is where we passed the test

The test of patience   The test of endurance
The test of letting go and letting God

The test of a lifetime

I think the trials were worth it though
We learned our strengths
Our weaknesses

Our ability to rely on each other

We stayed the course   We fought the fight

We let go : And let God

And He gave us time

We learned it together : At home

Sun Kisses.

The sun is streaming through the window to wake me

I feel the warmth on my cheek

It is as wonderful and comforting as your touch

I prefer to think of it as your wake up kiss

That works for me

Morning kisses

From you

To the sun

To me

Dates, Fruits and other vegetables.

Internet dating.
Some of my friends say - why don't I?
Excuse me? I don't think so

Have you MET some of the people out there?
Why do you think they're online to begin with hmmmm?

OK, maybe I'm just mean, Or maybe I'm just too picky
Or maybe I'm just not interested

You see: I'm married
Yup.
You are still with me.

It was a miracle we ever found one another
But then, you always said God brought us together.

Someone told me "you need someone to take care of you"

Obviously they don't know me well.

Do the words
"Leave me alone" not resonate? Hmm, Maybe I should date
At least once

I would bring every picture of you (I have BOXES) and tell
every story of you in my repertoire, bring every letter you
wrote. Every note...Every doodle

And then I would pack up and go back to our home

Where I am safe
Secure
Surrounded with memories
And content to be alone

The Diner.

The mission: going to a restaurant alone.
It is definitely one of those challenges that need to be
tackled.

Eating at home : No problem
Eating in a restaurant or diner with everyone else at tables of
2 or more?   Daunting.

Should I wear a sign on my chest "yes I am alone"
No, it's ok.   I can do this

I hear the theme song from "Rocky" in my head

Da dut dah! Da dut dah!

Start with a small place first : The diner!

I open the door, The waitress glances up
"how many?"
"One"
"booth or table honey?"
"Booth"
"what can I get you to drink"
"Coffee, High Octane"

She smiles

"I'll brew you a fresh pot. I'm Jamie"
"I'm Mary. Thanks Jamie"

"da dut dah! Da dut dah!"

Little Steps.

I seem to find it easier to do the big things
When I take little steps.

Like cleaning out a drawer of memories

Just take out the junk. Pile it all on the floor and begin to
separate

This is important! It's a piece of paper with your name on it.

It is not in your handwriting. It is just one of those little
notepads sent in the mail in an attempt to get you to donate
money to their organization. We never did donate
But it has your name on it, so I must save it.

What is this?
Oh, an empty matchbook. Generic. It must mean
something. Can't throw that away. I might remember why
we kept it

Eureka!
A tiny piece of paper with…
Wait, let me see
Yup!
I see a part of a word you wrote
Can't lose this.

Wait   What am I doing?

Take a deep breath and look at this pile.

Be brave
Pick up the matchbook
THROW IT AWAY!
Whew! That was harder than I thought

The notepad
Ummmmm Oh gosh!
This is hard

What to do … What to do

Toss it!

No, can't

Yes I can

Think
You did not donate to this group.
You did not write on this pad
You did not even LIKE this group

Throw it away if just for spite!

Actually, I think you wanted me to toss it when it came too.

But the piece of paper with your handwriting.
That goes into the "keeper" pile.
Put it in the old cigar box

Revisit it another day.

I feel the panic creeping up inside
as I look at the pile of stuff in the middle of the floor.

Scoop it up
Put it back in the drawer

I've done enough for today

It was a little step
The next one will be easier

I hope

Blue Skies and Green Lights.

It was a beautiful day The sky was Carolina Blue

You know, the really amazing tone of blue - the one that comes after a huge storm?

Yup
The perfect day to take a ride.

I head to the CTS. I filled it up last night in the event that the day would be perfect

House: locked
Dogs: fed
Cats: in charge

I put the key in "Michael Wayne" shows up on the personalized dashboard screen

"let's go for a ride LB"

Sunroof is open
Stereo: waiting to hit the road

I head to the back roads, the winding paths. The ones where maximum shifting is required. Thank God you wanted a 5-speed.

Open her up. Hit "Play"
Pink Floyd "Terminal Frost" thunders through the chassis
Here it comes, the sax solo

A jolt of energy hits my bloodstream as I take the corner

Between David Gilmour's guitar and the soaring sax
The road and the car become part of the music

When the album has finished
The next CD begins.
I hear the opening tune, press the forward button to
advance the tracks

The keyboards ring out

The skies are still blue,
But there is a more intense electrical storm inside of me.

My right hand clenches the stick shift as I feel yours beneath
mine.

"everything I do…I do it for you"

How many times had we cruised to those albums

How many times did you tell me,
"listen to the words, this is how I feel"
When that song came on

How many times did I place my hand over yours on that stick
shift
As I felt the meaning of every word, every phrase and every
note pass from you to me

Music always united us.

It's there for us still.

As the last power chord kicks in with the drums and the
keys, I feel my heart swell with joy and utter grief.

I knew this would affect me. But I needed to have it open
the portal to where you join me on a beautiful day
Of Blue Skies and Green Lights.

Sunrises with Michael.

I have begun to paint again

You had asked me for months before you died

"Honey, why aren't you painting?"

I told you I had to be in the right mood
Something had to inspire me

I had sketched some things on canvas
But never felt the need to paint.

You loved to see me paint

But then you would say
"Honey, when are you coming to bed?"
Because I would get caught up in magic.

My focus would be total

It was all I could do to stop and eat

It has been a while since I felt that way

Then today I picked up the photo your friend George sent
me where you were in Key West at sunrise

And it took me to the place of all those sunrises we shared

The ones we captured on film

The ones captured only in our hearts.

And I felt the need to put those moments on canvas

I thumbed through hundreds of photos

From Myrtle Beach
To Edisto Island
To Hawaii
To Alaska
To Wisconsin
To Virginia Beach
To Bermuda
And then finally
To Texas

The sunrises I wanted to capture were all on the water

The ocean

And the "little freshwater ocean-Lake Michigan"

I began to paint

The sunroom provided the perfect light
The smell of linseed oil and turpentine teased my nostrils

I love the smell of oils

Each moment came alive
As I relived them through the brush strokes.

Because Myrtle Beach was such a regular destination
It was captured in its various moods

I painted through the night-for days on end

The impulse was so strong and clear
I had no choice but to move with the moment

I could hear you saying
"Honey, when are you coming to bed"

"when I'm done my love…when I'm done"

I placed the brush in the can filled with brush cleaner

Swirled it around.

Took it out,
Wiped it on a paper towel.

Placed in on the side to dry
Took a deep breath

Then looked around

I smiled
I was surrounded by sunrises

I laughed
I remember each one clearly

Then I moved from canvas to canvas

Picked out one from Myrtle Beach:
Our last visit there

One from Edisto Island
The light that morning was amazing
It was a lovely day that ended in Charleston

One from Clear Lake, Texas
It was a picture you took that morning.
As you shot it with the 35mm film
I took pictures of you with the digital camera from the bed

You were silhouetted against the brilliant orange and gold
and red

But it was your shot that captured that moment of sunrise

I painted the beginning of the day through your eyes.

Those three I would keep.

They were the essence of our life together
One amazing sunrise after another

I felt a dampness on my cheek

Don't know if it was your tear or mine

Mostly likely both

I shook my head and looked around
The dogs were scattered around the room sound asleep

"let's go to bed puppies"

They perked up long enough to head with me into the
adjoining room

Time to sleep,

Another sunrise would come soon enough

I fell asleep with the smell of oil on my fingers, smudges on
my face
And a smile that was peace.

The Dynamic Duo.

Time to paint again
This time it is my favorite subject:

You

I've sketched you throughout the years

I've always loved your eyes.
They made me weak at the knees

"Bedroom eyes"

That eyebrow that would lift up to let me know you knew
what I was thinking: so John Belushi of you…

Expressive

And I always believed eyes were the key to the soul

I had painted you before, all rock and roll with your long
curling hair.

But this time, I wanted you and me
A portrait of whom we are together

Mostly a portrait of you

You are almost too easy to paint
I know your face better than my own

I see it in my mind and on every wall
The paint brush in my hand begins to move on its own-
propelled by memory

I feel as though I am bringing you alive again
Each brushstroke is a caress

You light the canvas

I feel your energy

And I feel your love

I see it in your eyes

In the way you smile

In the slant of your head as you look at me

I rush through the side that has me on it (I make my face
thinner-oh vanity) I don't really care how 'real' I am
This is not about me, or myself.
I am the afterthought

Because within the brushstrokes, I find it is you that I see

It is you that looks back at me.

And you speak to me through those eyes I love so dearly
and your quiet strength that lets me know:

All is well

You are ok

I am still loved

And you will always be there.

Midnight Sonata.

I bought a piano - It was a gift to me

I found one at an auction at a price I could not believe

It had a lovely tone-the tuner was quite impressed
I made room for it in a somewhat crowded space.

I sat down at the keyboard, the sheet music to Moonlight
Sonata stretched across the stand

I had just downloaded it from the internet, it was a song you
loved

Whenever we were near a piano, you sat down and played
the opening stanza.

It had been years since I had played that song.
I never had the affinity for it that you did

My fingers were stiff but I settled into the piece as I warmed
up

As the final notes rang into the night,
I lifted my hands from the keys and sat quietly.

How could I not realized how beautiful the song was?

And then I saw you.

Next to me on the piano bench
I could smell your skin, feel the texture of your shirt against
my cheek as I laid my head on your shoulder

"I miss you"

" I know, but I'm ok and I'll always be with you"

"I love you"

"I love you too. Gotta go"

"stay"

"you're ok. I'll see you again"

"counting on it"

And you melted into the night along with the notes

Rex came up next to me and nudged me with his nose.
He placed his paw on the bench
acknowledging you.

Maxx and Mikki had both appeared out of nowhere during
your visit and were staring at the empty place next to me.

I've heard animals are sensitive to spirits.

They knew you were there, and Maxx's tail drummed a
steady "thump thump thump" on the floor.

They all moved away as though following you:
then stopped.

A quiet whine came from Maxx's throat
And they all seemed to hang their heads in sadness.

But when they looked at me
I saw a light that had been missing

Each furry face was smiling

They pranced toward me as though to say
"did you see him, did you see him?!"

The quiet joy settled in the room for all of us.

I closed the piano

Fingered the sheet music

Next time

I think we'll try a duet.

The Boy Box.

Another number and name in the boy box
What is that? you ask

A box where the numbers and names are put

Names of men who are more boy than man,
but who think I should have their number "just in case"

I don't ask for them. They just give them to me.

"I noticed you when you walked in the room"

"Are you meeting someone"

I don't encourage them.

I humor them.

I humor me

The box has an impressive number of names inside
(If I do say so myself)
Flattered? Of course.

But I think you are getting a chuckle out of it as well

You'd say "they noticed your great legs darlin'"

Or my great shoes, which yes, show off my legs.

Hey, I'm not dead, the names just sit in the box until I decide
to toss them out

For now, they make me laugh and smile

Why not? At least they have good taste

The Park.

I've been working on our "Park" this spring.

That's what you called our yard after a few years.

When we first bought this house it was sitting in the middle
of a huge tract.

"Plunked down in a football field"
we would joke.

"you've got a great par 3 here" a friend told us…
the house makes it more challenging if you put the tee in
front
and the hole on the other side…
could even be a par 4…"

Neither of us were golfers and the thought of all that open
space,
well let's just say it wasn't our cup of "tee".

We started planting right away…

Little twigs most of them were

Certainly nothing with a trunk bigger than the size of my
thumb.

Then my parents came to visit, and we picked out trees and
shrubs - a gift to us from my siblings.

Dad helped me plant every one, and you and I marveled at
the transformation the larger plants made to the yard.

OK, they were still small:
the tallest tree was maybe 5 feet,

but they all had such POTENTIAL!

I bought some software that we could use to show the
landscaping I was doing, and you loved it when I showed
you the expected growth in 2, 5 and 10 years.

Oh the potential.

Suddenly it was 5 years,
and the twigs had become real trees…

The shrubs were shaping up nicely, and by 7 years,
you could no longer clearly see the house from the road.

You cut the lawn, and I trimmed and edged and bought
truckloads of pine straw to mulch the planting beds.

We had just finished for the day, went inside for dinner,
then came out to survey our work with fresh eyes.

"oh LB, you turned this into a PARK!"

Your eyes glowed with excitement and pleasure,
and your smile made my heart beat faster.

"Its beautiful"

It was! it was our park...our paradise….Our home….

Our Nest.

After our visit to Wing Haven earlier in the year,
we decided that someday our Park would have that same
splendor.

Albeit on a smaller scale.

Now I cut the grass, and I prefer to push the mower around the yard, as I can trim closer to the planted beds.

I have added a few more beds, and made more places to retreat to.

I keep in mind your amazement, your sense of wonder as I continue to work the land.

I lovingly tend to our park and talk to you as I move among our favorite trees.

Your mimosa took a big hit in the drought...
but it is in its' nature to pop up where ever it wants to,

And it wants very much to be in our park, so those little trees will be nurtured.

The little willow oak in front is no longer "little".

I trimmed the lower branches a few weeks ago,
and now I can walk under it without poking an eye out.
It now towers up over me, and has begun to cast a nice shade.

It has also become a home to the birds that have found food in the feeders, and water in the bowls.

They sing to me,

and give me peace.

As I walk through our park,
I hear echoes of our conversations,
punctuated by birdsong,
the whisper of wind in the trees,
the rustle of the pines,
and music from the chimes.

I inhale and close my eyes to pick up the fragrance of lilac,
sweet olive, roses, geraniums,
gardenias, magnolias, lilies,
clerodendrum, honeysuckle, a fig tree
and pine needles heated in the sun.

I talk to you as move through the spaces and secret places
that have been created out of a football field,

a useless par 4.

It is so much better than the computer graphics my Love

It is Our Park.

Meet you at the swing.

The Dance.

I pulled out some albums today.

The REAL albums.

Music on vinyl.

I played them loud enough to feel the vibrations move
through my lungs.

I closed my eyes and I danced.

I felt your hand at my back,
holding me close.

You were the only one I could dance with.

With you my feet were sure and graceful.

With eyes closed I was moving on emotion and clouds

And love

I purposefully played music that we had dipped and swayed
and clung to one another with.

The memories bring a smile that still lifts my heart to a place
of pure delight.

The dip was coming up…
I laughed out loud to the memory filled room.

The giggle started deep inside,
the sheer joy of what we had experienced was heady and
wonderful.

I considered allowing myself to dip, to fall,

but with eyes closed I did not want the rude awakening of crashing to the floor…

just in case you really were not there.

The song ends and I hear the low shush of the needle on vinyl.

Like a whisper in the night.

Comforting.

Warm.

Shush….shush….shush

A verbal

"I love you"

somewhere deep in the grooves.

I heard it….

I heard you.

I slowly open my eyes, the smile still on my lips.

I nod to the shadow in the darkened room.

I take a deep slow breath.

It was a wonderful dance my love.

I am content.

Hope.

Now that is the most *amazing* four-letter word!

It brings an involuntary smile to my face,
Lifts the spirit and lightens the pressure in my chest.
And provides a sense of true peace.

Hope

It comes from the oddest places
The certain knowledge that all is well and God will take care
of the minutia.

Hope

A full moon, a rainbow, the sun breaking through the clouds.
A single moment of peace .
Clarity from a mind usually clouded by a toxic fog

Hope

Knowing that the people you know and even more:
The people you don't know, are praying for God's grace to
shine your way.

Hope

Being able to truly trust the doctors making the most critical
of all decisions - And following their lead so closely you
dance together as if you are one.

Hope

The reason you can sleep at night, despite the fear.

Why each day is not sheer terror

But a day closer to salvation.

Hope

God's gift of light in the dark.

Epilogue

Years have passed since the day you left this earth.
Despite it all, the sun still rises.

Every day is a new adventure to explore.
Every moment I breathe in is precious.

Every person I encounter has value and worth

I have learned how much I treasure my friendships.

They have made me stronger,
The experiences have made me wiser.

I discovered some simple truths,
with you and without you:

It is the effort we make to connect with others that heal the
wounded, sad souls : including our own.
Personal joy is always within reach.

Hope is not a saying: it is a reality that you create.

The adventure of life and love continues....

I am laughing more than I have in years.

I learned that I really am a fierce, brave survivor to the core.

That my heart has room for more joy as long as I continue to
let faith, kindness and music fill my soul

'
and NEVER forget how to dance!

And I know our love survives in its special way

Forever Plus One Day

ABOUT THE AUTHOR

20 year Radio veteran, Mary London
was a well respected rock and roll DJ,
Music Director and Program Director
who shared her love of music and music
trivia with listeners. Her interviewing skills
were as legendary as her passion for the
music was audible. When the radio industry
changed, she took a new direction and DJ
became a voice actor and freelance copy-
writer. She booked and managed bands on
a local and regional level, and released two
metal compilations albums that were well
received in Europe on radio and in the metal
press. She worked with talented musicians
in jazz and blues. She has never stepped
away from her love of music and remains
active in the music industry today.

Although music has been her first career
love, writing has played no small role. She drew upon her skills to dream up
radio skits, applied the creative juices to bios and press kits for her bands.
Later it evolved into unique concepts designed for radio, TV and print
advertising campaigns for clients when she formed her ad agency Londonvox
Productions Inc. A natural mimic, she continues to use her vocal expertise on
national, regional and local campaigns. A savvy audio editor and producer,
she has a knack for theatre of the mind. Her ease with words led her to
express her innermost thoughts with the death of her husband Michael. It
became her salvation as she put her pen to paper to voice the loss of her soul-
mate.

"The Loss World" is a personal journey through grief and growth.

*" As I began to make my way through the fog,
I read some of what I had written and thought
perhaps it could help others to move forward
with their memories intact. No apologies for
missing what we've lost!
Learning that we can wake up and take a step
without wanting to crumble is imperative.*

*This is not a self- help book. It is a self - awareness journal. My goal
was to heal myself, and share my healing. I have been told it is an
incredibly personal story.*